To a great dad!
With love,

_____

_____

Date: _____

Blessings for you, Dad

© 2012 Christian Art Gifts, RSA
        Christian Art Gifts Inc., IL, USA

Designed by Christian Art Gifts

Images used under license from Shutterstock.com

Scripture quotations are taken from the New King James Version.
Copyright © 1979, 1980, 1982 by Thomas Nelson, Inc. Used by permission.
All rights reserved.

Printed in China

ISBN 978-1-4321-0245-6

12   13   14   15   16   17   18   19   20   21   –   11   10   9   8   7   6   5   4   3   2

Blessings *for you,* DAD

ANGUS BUCHAN

From an early age **Angus Buchan** felt God's calling on his life to spread the gospel.

Angus began to fulfill this calling in 1980 when he started Shalom Ministries. He has transformed the lives of thousands of people in amazing ways through the Mighty Men Conferences held on his farm *Shalom*. He has proven that God can do extraordinary things through ordinary people if they choose to follow Him.

A passionate preacher at Christian gatherings and on TV, Angus also made his debut as a best-selling author with *Faith Like Potatoes* – a powerful testimony of his unwavering faith in God. He is a full-time evangelist and sought-after speaker at local and international events.

Angus lives with his wife, Jill, on their farm in the KwaZulu-Natal Midlands. They have been blessed with five adult children who love and serve the Lord.

Foreword

Fatherhood is a great privilege and honor bestowed on us by God.

Please never take it for granted that you are a father. I do not know how many men are praying who are unable to father children. It is a great responsibility to hold this office. We are living in an era where we are faced with a fatherless generation. I trust that this book will encourage you to take up your rightful status as prophet, priest and king, first and foremost in your own family, then in your business and finally in the community.

God is looking for men to whom He can entrust this responsibility. In second Chronicles 16:9 the Bible says, "For the eyes of the LORD run to and fro throughout the whole earth, to show Himself strong on behalf of those whose heart is loyal to Him." This is you and me.

Keep up the good work and remember you are not alone. You have many brothers in Christ who are holding the same responsibility.

– Angus Buchan

Help your children to walk
in the footsteps of Jesus.
Instruct and teach them to
love the Lord their God.

You were called,
because Christ also suffered for us,
leaving us an example,
that you should follow His steps.

1 Pet. 2:21

It's not how much
you give your children.
What's important is that
they know that you love them.

If you want your children to reach
great heights, it's not going to be
through extra lessons, or extra coaching;
it's going to be through affirmation.

Let everything that we do today **bring glory** to Jesus Christ.

Whatever you do, do it heartily,
as to the Lord and not to men.

Col. 3:23

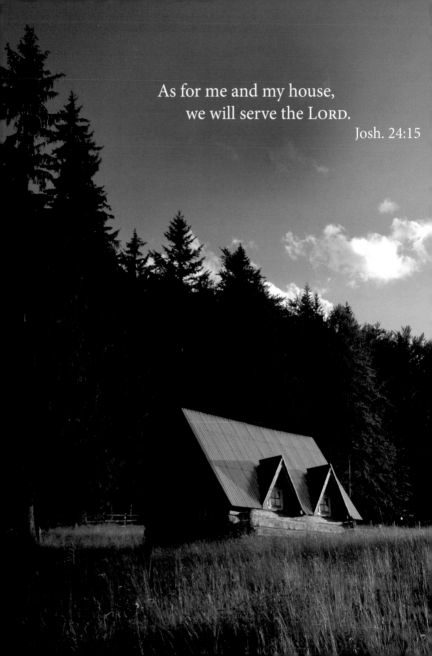

As for me and my house,
we will serve the LORD.

Josh. 24:15

The Lord never designed us
to be on our own.
We need each other,
just like iron sharpening iron,
just like the coal needs the fire
in order to burn brightly.
Guard your relationship
with your fathers,
and with your sons,
with passion and purpose.

If you are living a godly life and walking in the ways of Jesus Christ, you can rest assured that when your children grow up and leave school and make their way in life, they will imitate you.

The father is the head of the home;
the mother is the heart of the home;

the children are the reward,
the joy and the life of the home.

This is what God expects
fathers and sons to do for each other.
To stand with each other,
not just in times of success
but in times of crisis,
in times of supposed defeat.
But, most of all, on a daily basis,
just to affirm them and tell them
how much they mean to you.

Be strong and of good courage;
do not be afraid, nor be dismayed,
for the LORD your God
is with you wherever you go.
Josh. 1:9

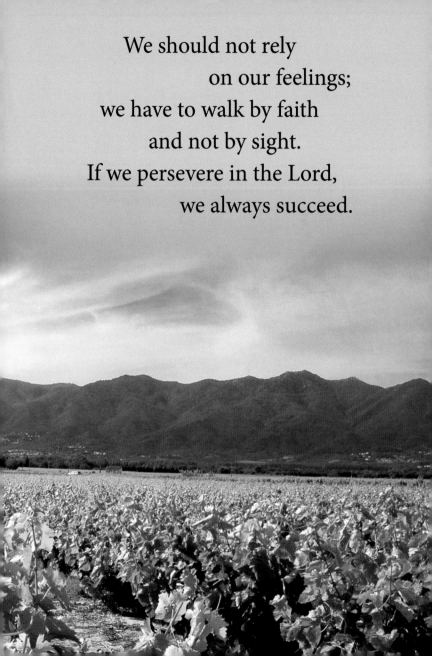

Lead your children
to have a living experience
and a relationship
with Jesus Christ
as their Lord
and Savior.

Time is of the essence.
Before you know it your children
will be grown up.

What will you choose today:
quality time, quantity
time, or both?

Be of good courage,
and He shall strengthen your heart,
all you who hope in the LORD.

Ps. 31:24

Be of good courage.

Get up today mighty man of God,
and in courage go forth to face the world.
The Lord has promised that

He will strengthen our hearts.

Put Jesus' principles
first in your life,
your family and your business.
And God will do the rest!

How wonderful
when the whole family
can worship together.

Respect your father
and your mother.
It's the first commandment
in the Bible with
a promise added to it.

"Honor your father
and your mother,
as the LORD your God has
commanded you,
that your days may be long,
and that it may be well
with you in the land which the
LORD your God is giving you."

Deut. 5:16

A great way to ensure
that your children
know and love the Lord
is to have regular
quiet times together.

Don't worry about
what tomorrow brings.
Don't be concerned
about yesterday, because it's gone.
Enjoy the moment, today!
Seize the day with your family.

The fruit that people are looking for
is your character.
The greatest compliment that
you'll ever get from any man
is when he can say to you,

"I see that you've
been walking with God."
That comes from spending
time with Him.

We are called
as men to be the
**prophets, priests,
and kings
in our home.**
If we want our home
to run in an orderly manner,
that's exactly what
we've got to be.

God created your children
as unique people.

Love them
for who they are.

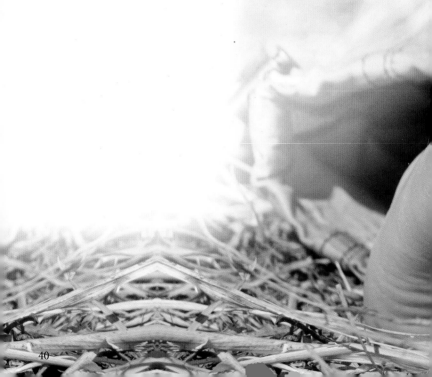

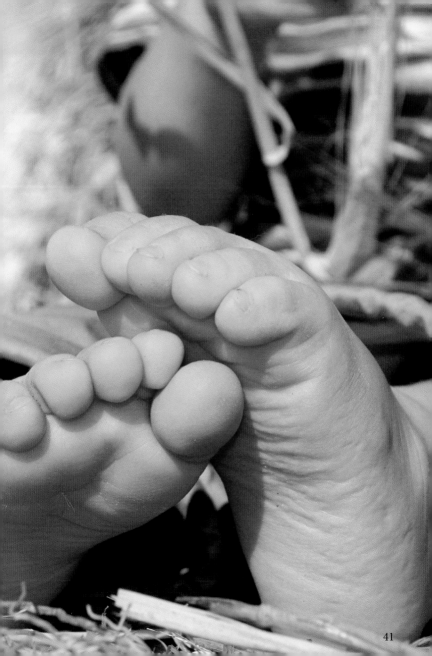

Being a father
is a tremendous
responsibility.

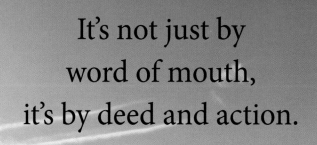

It's not just by
word of mouth,
it's by deed and action.

God is the past, the present, the future.

The family unit is God's number one priority. It's more important to Him than nations, education, inventions, advancement.

As the father,
as the man of the house,
you have a responsibility to make sure
that your home, your household
is running according to God's mandate,
according to God's commandments
and not anyone else's.

This is the day the LORD has made;
we will rejoice and be glad in it.

Ps. 118:24

Remember,

the Lord promised you

that He will be faithful

to you and that

He will supply

all of your needs

according to

His riches
in glory.

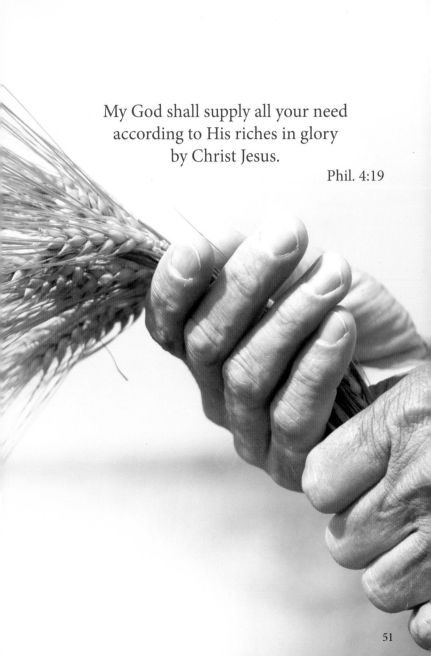

My God shall supply all your need
according to His riches in glory
by Christ Jesus.

Phil. 4:19

To fulfill
your calling as father,
never take your eyes
off Jesus. Press on.
Run the race.
Fight the good fight.
You can, for you have Jesus
with you always.

Turn to God,
love one another,
have patience with one another,
and honor one another.

Don't look at your problem,
look at your Problem Solver,
and that mountain will become
a mere molehill.

"Assuredly, I say to you, if you have faith
as a mustard seed, you will say to this mountain,
'Move from here to there,' and it will move;
and nothing will be impossible for you."
Matt. 17:20

Encourage your children.

It doesn't matter what they're going through; see them through God's eyes as God would see them. Believe for that miracle. Believe for that turn-around. Believe for their salvation. Start seeing them as God sees them and you'll find that suddenly the whole situation will turn.

Those who wait on the LORD
shall renew their strength;
they shall mount up with
wings like eagles,
they shall run and not be weary,
they shall walk and not faint.

Isa. 40:31

Just like a little fledgling eagle steps
out of the nest into fresh air and
starts to fly like his mother and father,
step out today and start to fly.
You will have such a life as you never
dreamed possible.

It is good to know that there is One who is faithful and true, who will never leave us nor forsake us.

He is the Good Shepherd.

Jesus Christ Himself.

The Good Shepherd

remains faithful and stands in the door

of the fold and will not allow any intruder in.

God will never fail you, or your family, or let you down.

"I am the good shepherd. The good shepherd gives His life for the sheep."

John 10:11

God loves you with all of His heart,
mind, soul and strength.
What He wants is for you to go and do
the same, and serve others as
He has served you.

God bless you today as you go out,
running with purpose,
with the finish line in sight.

Let us run with endurance
the race that is set before us.
Heb. 12:1

Jesus Christ
is a miracle-working God.
He transforms men's lives from being

fearful, totally incompetent,

full of anger, hatred,

and mostly fear, into men of stature;

men of love, power,

and a sound mind.

This is our inheritance.

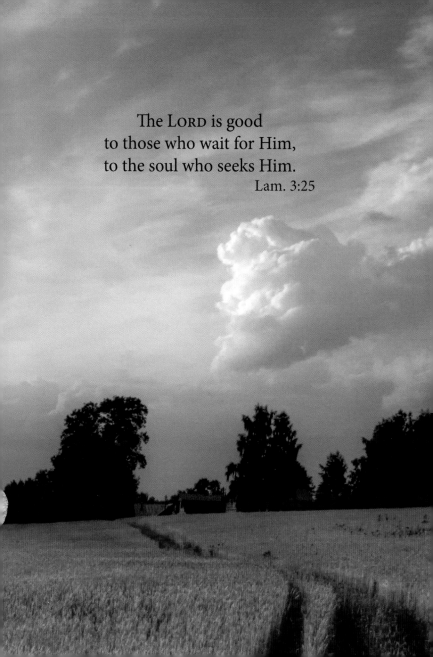

The LORD is good
to those who wait for Him,
to the soul who seeks Him.
Lam. 3:25

A family that prays together
stays together.

Jesus holds the family unit
closer to His heart
than anything else.

"I will be a Father to you,
and you shall be My sons and daughters,"
says the Lord Almighty.

2 Cor. 6:18

Every new frontier
can become
a new opportunity.

Delight yourself also in the LORD,
and He shall give you the desires of your heart.

Ps. 37:4

Children
are a heritage
from the Lord,
a reward
from Him.

Let God establish you
to be the man that He wants
you to be in your home!

Encourage your children all the time.
Love them, protect them, lead them
and teach them that
God loves them and cares for them.

Teach your children to love
and trust God, and they will
never turn from Him.

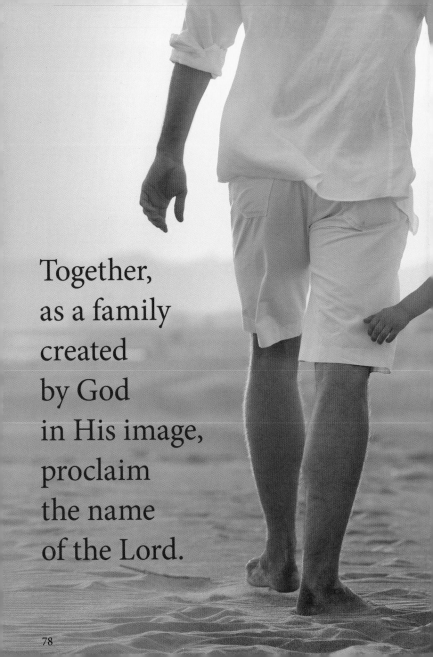

Together,
as a family
created
by God
in His image,
proclaim
the name
of the Lord.

As you go out into the world today,

know that God goes with you.

You have nothing to fear.

God is totally and absolutely

trustworthy.